Heating
and
Cooling

How Do Things Change?

Written by Kerrie Shanahan

Series Consultant: Linda Hoyt

WorldWise™
Content-based Learning

Contents

Introduction

Dinner is being prepared.

Some foods are heated, and some are cooled. But, whatever we do to these foods, they are changed.

What are these changes and how do they happen?

And after the food is heated or cooled, can it be changed back to the way it was?

Chapter 1
Changing by heating

Most foods change when they are heated. Sometimes, when they change, the foods are very different – and sometimes, the change that happens can never be undone.

Popcorn

What happens when corn kernels are heated?

When corn kernels are heated, they change.

They now look very different. They change colour and shape, they smell different, they feel different and you can eat them.

What happened?

When the corn kernels were heated, they changed and became something new – popcorn.

The popcorn will never change back to corn kernels.

This change cannot be undone.

Eggs

What happens when an egg is cooked?

When an egg is cooked, it changes.

If you boil or fry an egg, the egg looks very different. The clear part of the egg turns white, it is firmer and it smells different.

The cooked egg looks the way it does because of how it was cooked.

Will eggs cooked in these different ways, taste the same? What else will be different?

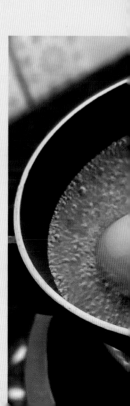

What happened?

When the egg was heated, or cooked, it changed and became something new.

The egg will never change back. It is impossible to change a cooked egg back into a raw egg.

The heat has changed it forever.

Bread

What happens when a slice of bread is heated?

When bread is toasted, it changes.

The bread looks and feels different. It is darker, it is harder and it smells different. It is now called toast.

Does bread taste the same as toast? How are they different?

What happened?

When the bread was toasted, it changed and became something new.

The toast will never change back. It is impossible to change a piece of toast back into a piece of bread.

Chapter 2

Changing back again

Some foods and drinks that change when they are heated or cooled can change back when they cool down or warm up.

Water

What happens to water when it is frozen?

When water is frozen, it becomes ice.

What will happen when ice is taken out of the freezer and starts to warm up? Will it change?

Will the water be the same as it was before it was frozen? Will it taste the same?

What happened?

When the ice was taken out of the freezer, it changed back into water – back to the way it was before.

Freezing water is a change that can be undone, or **reversed**.

13

Chocolate

What happens to chocolate when it is heated?

When chocolate is heated, it melts and becomes soft and runny.

How is the chocolate the same? How is it different? Will it taste the same as it did before it was heated and cooled?

What happens when the chocolate cools down? Does it change?

What happened?

When the chocolate melted, it was still chocolate. When it cooled, it changed back to the way it was before.

This change can be undone, or reversed.

15

Chapter 3

What is the same and what is different?

Let's **investigate** some other foods.

What happens when they are heated?

What happens when they are **frozen**?

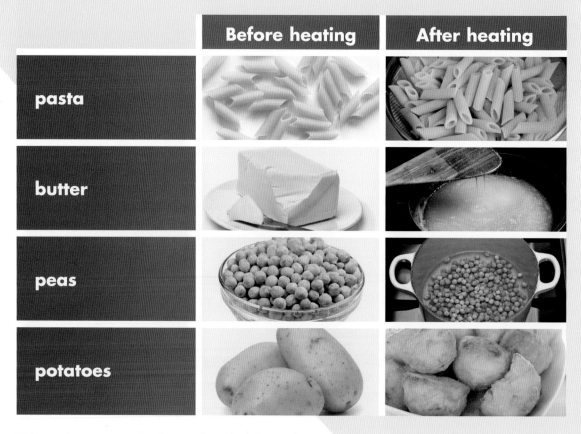

	Before heating	After heating
pasta		
butter		
peas		
potatoes		

What happens to these foods after they are heated?

Do they change? How?

Can they be changed back?

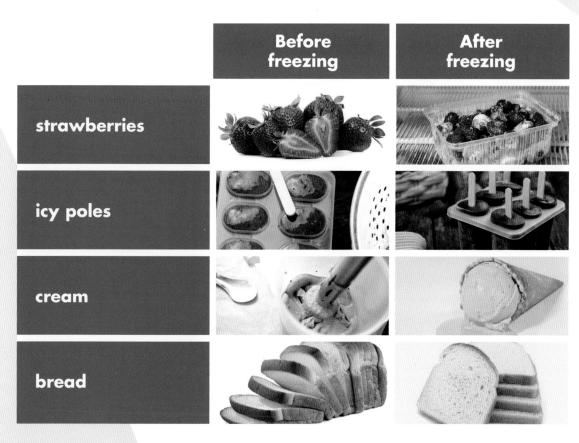

	Before freezing	After freezing
strawberries		
icy poles		
cream		
bread		

What happens to these foods after they are frozen?

Do they change? How?

Can they be changed back?

Conclusion

Changing the **temperature** of foods and drinks by heating or cooling them can make them change. Often, they will look different, smell different, feel different and taste different.

Sometimes, these changes cannot be **reversed**. They cannot be changed back to the way they were.

But sometimes, these changes can be undone. Heating or cooling these foods and drinks can change them back to the way they were.

Glossary

frozen something that has been cooled so much, that it has become solid

investigate to find out by studying, questioning and/or observing

kernels the small, individual parts found on a corn cob

reversed changed back to the way something originally was

temperature how hot or cold something is

Index